I AM AN INTROVERT

The Power of Introverts and Introverted Leadership

BY JOSHUA MOORE

By Joshua Moore

FREE DOWNLOAD

INSIGHTFUL GROWTH STRATEGIES FOR YOUR PERSONAL AND PROFESSIONAL SUCCESS!

amazonkindle   nook   kobo   iBooks

Windows   android   BlackBerry

Sign up here to get a free copy of The Growth Mindset book and more:
www.frenchnumber.net/growth

TABLE OF CONTENTS

By Joshua Moore

Introduction

The word "introvert" is a combination of two Latin words: intro, meaning inward and vertere, meaning turning. A person who is introverted, then, is someone who "turns inward" for all their sources of energy rather than seeking energy from external sources.

Think about those two sentences for a moment. What could be more powerful than the ability to recharge from within? If I were writing about technology rather than human beings, and I described an introverted cell phone that was about to go on the market, I can pretty much guarantee I would instantly have the world's attention.

I believe that the enormous potential for self-sourced power that introverts possess is exactly WHY society has given them the reputation of being shy, reticent souls who prefer to be alone. While being shy, being private and enjoying one's own company may be characteristics of some people who are introverts, these qualities shouldn't and don't define who they are and what they are capable of accomplishing! Our society depends on external motivations, inspirations, and aspirations to thrive. Introverts are the antithesis of this superficial co-dependent environment, and so society has defined them in terms chosen to downplay and demean their powerful gifts.

My intention in writing this book is twofold. I

want to deconstruct the traditional stereotypical definition of the introvert, exploring the different types of introversion, as well as their individual advantages and disadvantages. I then want to help introverts to implement and utilize their unique self-sourced gifts in order to overcome their fears, give them protection from the challenges of existing in an extrovert-centric society, and allow them to accomplish personal and professional life goals, including those of relationship, leadership, and entrepreneurship. Please join me on this eye-opening journey and we will shatter some myths and redefine what being an introvert really means.

Part One

Introversion: The STAR that is lit from within

I would like to begin this section by exploring four different types of introversion, helping you to figure out which type, or which combination of types you are. For years, any introvert who didn't comply with the stereotypical definition of the shy, retiring, loner was given the name "complicated" introvert. I don't know about you, but this term reminds me of the Facebook relationship status: It's Complicated, meaning, well... who knows? There are actually 4 specific types of introverts according to Jonathan Cheek, a recognized academic, researcher and psychologist. They are:

- Social Introverts
- Thinking Introverts
- Anxious Introverts
- Restrained Introverts

The very names of these types of introversion are quite descriptive, but before I delve into the details of each, I would like you to take the following simple test to determine which of these types you most resonate with.

Which STAR are you? (TEST)

Q1. You are invited to a big party at a popular local club. As the day approaches you:

A. Still intend on going, but make sure two or three of your close friends are attending as well.

B. Have to remind yourself about it as you keep forgetting because you are in the middle of writing an article for a magazine.

C. Start to dread what seemed like a fun idea initially. You really hope a great excuse for NOT going materializes soon!

D. Will most likely go, but have planned ahead for breaks from all the noise and distraction. No doubt, at one point you'll take a nice walk and hopefully find a quiet corner to chat with your partner or a close friend about the home beer brewing kit you've been experimenting with at home for the last month.

Q2. The meeting you are going to today requires that you verbally present for 10 minutes:

A. You will be fine, but will look forward to relaxing by yourself at home later in the day.

B. You will come prepared with a written synopsis to hand out to everyone and which you can refer to from time to time, so you don't lose your original train of thought.

C. You wake up with a stomach ache. The only thing worse than the actual presentation will be later when you mentally review every stupid awkward thing you said and did.

D. You are happy that the meeting is in the afternoon when you are more alert. You will remind yourself to take your time and not get flustered because you are only supposed to speak for 10 minutes...

Q3. Your best friend has asked you to be the maid of honor/best man at his/her wedding:

A. You will do a great job because this is your best friend, but you also understand that these next months will require lots of carefully scheduled alone time so that you can appreciate being in the moment during the more hectic, social times.

B. You're going to need lots of post-its and phone reminders to make sure things get done. It's a good thing they know you and will understand if sometimes you get confused or lose your train of thought. That's why they love you!

C. You want to do this for your friend, but you also wonder at times how your best friend could do this to you!

D. You will need to clear your schedule and make a detailed, thorough plan of attack. Also, if you are going to be in charge, things will have to be the way you need them to be. You care a great deal, but you don't want this to get out of hand!

Q4.You have been asked out on a date by a co-worker who you are interested in:

A. You are excited. Finally, you'll get to spend some one-on-one time with this interesting, attractive person!

B. You are very happy. You hope they don't want too much input on the date itself, though, because you kind of just like to float along...

C. You are excited but increasingly apprehensive. You try not to project what could go wrong and are annoyed with yourself that weirdly, you'd be ok if they canceled.

D. You accept after thinking carefully about it. You also think and communicate about the details of the date. This is important to you, and you want it to be successful.

Q5. You go to a comedy club with a friend. One of the comedians picks you out to interact with:

A. Not your favorite thing, but you'll get through it. Thank God tomorrow you don't have any plans!

B. You don't notice you've been picked on until your friend taps you on the shoulder. You've been daydreaming about being a stand-up comedian who has to tell jokes to aliens...

C. Aughhhhh...You. Are. Dying. Later, you'll replay the horror over and over on a mental loop as you lie awake.

D. You take a deep breath. Think about what you're going to say...then politely decline to take part, suggesting they pick someone who is funny.

Q6. Your son is on a soccer team, and it's your turn to work in the refreshment stand during the game:

A. You volunteer to run the grill. It's a solitary job that will require your attention and people will be grateful that you are good at it and will keep the small talk to a minimum.

B. You volunteer to restock the plastic utensils and condiment packages. Then you can keep to yourself and think about that research challenge you were assigned last week.

C. You get stressed out thinking about it and by the time you get there, you do whatever you are told, awkwardly interacting with customers and other parents for two endless hours until you are finally set free.

D. You volunteer to dismantle and clean the Slurpee machine, which you have become an expert at. You enjoy the work and are more than happy to discuss what you are doing with anyone who might be interested.

Q7. You have volunteered for the upcoming local election. Instead of giving you letters to write as you requested, they have assigned you to make cold calls on the telephone:

A. You care about this candidate, so you make the phone calls, following the script and fulfilling your duty of making 100 calls. You celebrate by turning off ALL the technology around you and sitting by the pool enjoying the solitude.

B. You start off making the phone calls, but keep rambling on and going off track, so that you are reassigned to your original letter writing request!

C. You call in, feigning illness, which, in a way, is true...

D. You politely but firmly show the coordinator your volunteer form which clearly states that you are volunteering to write letters.

Q8. You have been chosen to interview for a new job which would result in a promotion

and a pay raise. The interview will consist of a one on one interview and a follow-up interview by the board of directors:

A. You are fine with the one-on-one interview. After all, you were recruited to interview for this job, so that means there is already interest in you. You maintain your composure for the group interview, promising yourself uninterrupted alone time during the weekend.

B. You bring examples of your work, letting them speak for you throughout the process. Interviews and verbal communication, in general, are not your strong suit but you know your work stands on its own.

C. You try and deny that dark voice in your psyche that keeps taunting you with the absurd possibility that you were chosen to interview for this job by mistake! You white-knuckle it through the process, then have to call in sick the next day because of the stress induced migraine you've given yourself.

D. You prepare for this multi-challenging day thoroughly. You are passionate about your work and enjoy discussing it in your own time and manner. As long as the schedule is adhered to and there are no surprises you will do well.

Q9. You are at a business conference and are introduced to 3 people during a break, then left to talk to them:

A. You've been to this rodeo before. You trot out a well-used one liner or joke, chat a bit about the last speaker and then make your excuses and exit.

B. You're not quite sure what just happened. The person you knew has left. You shrug your shoulders, laugh a bit and wander away...

C. You overshare because you have been caught in a stressful situation and ramble on until the conversation peters out to an awkward silence, whereupon you back away, tripping over someone behind you.

D. You listen carefully to the conversation, and if you feel you have something pertinent to add, you do so, thoughtfully and thoroughly.

Q10. You are sitting in the window seat of a half empty bus, and someone not only sits next to you but initiates small talk!

A. You chat politely for a few minutes, then take out your trusty emergency book and start to read.

B. You engage in conversation but keep losing the thread, and have to ask the person to repeat themselves or make up a response that you hope makes some sort of sense.

C. You pretend you are asleep, even though your heart is pounding and you can't catch your breath. Alternately, you ring the bell for the bus stop and exit, 5 miles away from your original destination.

D. You listen to what the other person is saying. If they interest you, you engage. If they don't, you politely tell them that you need to rest before your next activity.

Q11. You are about to enter what you think is an empty elevator, but as you get on you realize there is another passenger.

A. You acknowledge their presence, press your floor and retire into your personal bubble.

B. You wander into the elevator, as your shirt sleeve gets caught in the closing door, disengage and continue to fantasize about time travel.

C. You immediately take out your cell phone and become mesmerized by yelp.

D. You take a deep breath, nod politely and solemnly
read the emergency exit information on the wall to yourself.

Q12. As part of a professional development day, you have been broken up into groups and need to perform a skit demonstrating the

skills you have been taught!

A. You knew this was coming because you read the syllabus as soon as you walked in this morning. You take the path of least resistance, playing a minor role.

B. You volunteer to write a haiku that sums up the skit in 17 syllables, which you will recite at the end.

C. You didn't read the syllabus. You have a panic attack. You volunteer to be the scribe, or make props or run the computer or give up your firstborn...

D. You listen carefully, volunteer to be the narrator and introduce the skit with a thoughtful introduction.

Q13. You are at a work picnic and have managed to get away from the crowd and are sitting under a tree near the lake thoroughly enjoying yourself. A group comes along and "outs" you, asking what you are doing:

A. You respond with a smile and small talk, i.e., "isn't it great here", etc. and hopefully in a few minutes they will move on.

B. You are deep in your thoughts and don't notice them until you hear the sound of laughter...

C. You lie and tell them you are meeting someone there. You then pantomime looking for them, feeling like a fool.

D. You tell them you are taking a break from the day and enjoying the solitude of being under a tree by the lake.

Q.14. You are starting your own business and attend a business development event at the local tulip festival:

A. You walk around, participate in the silent auction, eat and drink and speak if spoken to. You gather brochures from other businesses and consider it a productive evening.

B. You are drawn to specific booths that resonate with your own business ideas. You interact with kindred spirits and make potential business contacts.

C. You try and make small talk, but you can't seem to infiltrate the cliques at this event. You spend two hours wandering around and end up not making a single contact. You are bitter and relieved.

D. You visit each booth and carefully peruse their exhibits and materials. If you want more information you ask about it. There is one business which really interests you. You end up talking to the owner for over an hour and agree to meet up again and share information.

Q15. Your grandmother has made you promise you will take her to the annual family reunion where there will be at least

100 relatives you've never met:

A. You prepare yourself, getting lots of sleep, and psyching yourself up for the event. Gram will conk out on the long car ride home, and you'll get to refuel then.

B. You spend the day with the oldest members, who don't seem to care if you aren't always paying attention or watching the antics of the youngest who don't care at all!

C. You go in a funk and end up getting into a fight with Grandma who keeps trying to ditch you with stranger cousins...

D. You study the family tree in preparation and meet up with a cousin who shares your interest in ancestry.

Q16. Your kid sister has begged you to take her to a music festival. It's in a huge muddy field, jam packed with barefooted humanity:

A. You set up detailed meeting places and times and basically shutdown in between, trying to focus on the music or happier, quieter times.

B. You end up getting lost, and your kid sister has to find YOU!

C. You lose a shoe in the mud in the first 5 minutes and spend two days, wet, deaf and miserable. Your kid sister says you ruined the trip and she's never speaking to you again, which is your only consolation!

D. You bring ear plugs, books, a professional adventurer's tent, a blow-up mattress and solar powered lights, set up camp and settle in for some serious reading time.

Q.17. It's Christmas time, and you've waited till the last minute to do your shopping. You're in a shopping mall full of lights, noise, music, and irate shoppers:

A. You have only yourself to blame. You march in, armed with your list and muscle through the crowds until you've done all your shopping. You escape to your gloriously quiet car and vow you will plan better next year.

B. You wander around in a daze until you feel a bit car sick. You are inspired to go home and paint a picture of what you have just experienced. You scan the finished work of art, print up boxes of cards, and gift your family and friends with them.

C. You grit your teeth and go into the fray, impulse buying as fast as you can. You return home in a deep preholiday depression and weep quietly as you survey the collection of junk you've just purchased for your loved ones.

D. You stop at the entrance and decide you aren't up to the punishment of the day. You return home and write thoughtful apology letters to your family and friends and offer to shovel driveways and sidewalks as a useful and solitary New Year's gift.

Q18. Your mother has set you up on a blind date:

A. You know she means well and is only thinking about future grandchildren, so you suck it up and give it your best shot. Who knows? Maybe trial by fire will do the trick.

B. You get the address wrong and go to the wrong venue. When you ask a nice person for directions home, you end up chatting, s/he finds your absentmindedness enchanting, and you end up making a date for next Tuesday!

C. You agree to the date, spend the next week and half stressing out about it, stand the date up at the last minute and spend the rest of the night wondering why you always end up ALONE.

D. You interrogate your mother on said date, and, if her answers intrigue you, you go on said date with the intention of meeting and getting to know a person who could become integral to your future.

Q19. Your new work-from-home job is a dream come true, but the one downside is you have to conduct a majority of your business on the telephone:

    A. You work out a schedule in your head, clearly defining what percentage of your day and what time of your day you will spend on the phone. This way you can experience a beginning, middle, and end to this undesirable aspect and truly appreciate the solitude of the rest of your day.

    B. You keep the phone work to a bare minimum, and focus on the more visual, written and creative side of your job, earning a reputation as a gifted expert in your field so that eventually you will be paid solely for what you are good at and deemed too valuable to waste your time on the phone.

    C. You project your feelings about the phone work, making it the focal point of each day. You forget how nice it is to be working from home, and end up wishing you were back in an office environment where at least you were used to the routine.

    D. You carefully script your phone conversations and keep to your message points. This allows you more productive time to do the work at home that you truly love.

Q20. It's Monday morning, and your office mate asks you what you did over the weekend:

A. You tell her, but it makes you feel slightly claustrophobic. This is why you don't like small talk. It doesn't mean anything.

B. You try to explain why what you did was so important to you, but you stop when you see her eyes glaze over. She just doesn't get you...

C. It doesn't matter because whatever you did won't make sense to her and she'll just end up making you feel bad because it sounds like you don't have any friends.

D. You're really not a morning person, so you try to keep things short and sweet. Unfortunately, she takes this as abruptness and arrogance.

Q21. I feel truly inspired by:

A. Meaningful conversations with one or two other people. I could talk all night with the right small group!

B. Things I see in nature or art or films and how thinking about them fills me with creativity and ideas.

C. People who don't judge me; who take the time and have the patience to really get who I am and what I'm passionate about.

D. People who listen to me as well as I listen to others. People who share my passion, expertise and knowledge.

I truly enjoy social activities that include:

A. Time to socialize as a group and time to break off into smaller groups or even go off by myself without people thinking I'm being moody.

B. Creative time to think, dream and visualize, followed by time to share!

C. Kind of an open door policy so that I can come and go as I please and not feel as if I have to spend a certain amount of time in order not to appear rude.

D. Spending time doing and talking about the things that are important to me with people who have the same passions. I love the give and take of social interactions like this!

Q22. I don't mind having to speak in public:

A. When I am prepared and know in advance that afterward, I will have ample time to refuel by myself.

B. If I feel comfortable with my audience; i.e., if they accept me for who I am and are interested in my unique point of view. It might be a good idea to remind me about when and where I need to be though!

C. As long as I know exactly what is expected from me. No last minute changes, no substitutions, no pressure to do or say anything I'm not prepared to say or do!

D. When I get to speak about something I am passionate about, and I have an audience who feels the same way. I'm reticent, not shy!

Q23. The thing that upsets me the most about how people react to my introversion is:

A. When they think I don't like to be with people. That's so far off the mark. I just need equal time to myself.

B. When they are disappointed in me or think I'm weird. I love creating and making things for people to react to. Without people to react to what I make, it's all meaningless. But when people feel let down or judge me because I'm different...I can't handle it.

C. When they get mad at me because I don't always follow through. I wish they understood how crippling it is to literally feel scared to death at the thought of being out in a crowd. Sometimes I just need a little extra patience and understanding.

D. When they think I am unfeeling or cold because I don't share their interests. Although I can be serious and intense, I have deep feelings for people, and once you gain my trust you also gain my undying loyalty!

Tally up your responses and see which letter the majority of your answers fell under. A equals Social Introvert; B equals Thinking Introvert; C equals Anxious Introvert and D equals Restrained Introvert. Let's now explore each of these categories in more depth, as well as list their specific advantages and disadvantages.

The Social Introvert: The social introvert probably comes closest to the popular idea of what all introverts are. Social Introverts prefer socializing with small groups, rather than large ones when they are in the mood to socialize at all. Often though, they prefer solitude. This does not mean they are shy or anxious around other people. The very act of being social drains energy and exhausts the social introvert. They need alone time to refuel their energy. They have a finite amount of energy for socializing in groups or at parties or bars. When that energy is depleted, they need to go into quiet observation mode immediately. Unfortunately, when non-introverts see them go into this mode, they often misinterpret it as a change in mood. They judge the introvert as suddenly being angry or sad or moody. This could not be further from the truth, but like anyone else, if the introvert continues to be questioned about their sudden change in "attitude", they may indeed become frustrated or irritated! Likewise, when a social introvert schedules alone-time specifically to refuel, and non-introverts assume they are being stood up or blown off, the introvert can feel hurt and misunderstood. For this reason, it is integral for the social introvert to have one or two true friends who understand and accept their need for periods of solitude. Social introverts are adept at compensation techniques, scheduling time alone and timing social events, The most important thing non-introverts need to understand about social introverts is that they are not mercurial, moody or difficult people who "go off" others at the drop of a hat. They merely run out of social steam, much like a car stops running when it runs out of gas. We don't think the car is mad at us or being snobby because it has stopped running. We should give the social introvert the same basic understanding!

Advantages of Being a Social Introvert:

- Because social introversion is not fueled by anxiety, inner thought processes or personality, it is most likely the most "acceptable" form of introversion in our society.
- Sudden loss of social energy can be pre-empted by careful planning.
- Scheduling of solitary "refueling" time ensures enough social energy when desired or needed.

- The gift of truly enjoying being alone can never be overestimated. There are many people in our society who cannot bear being by themselves for even a short amount of time and will put up with less than the desirable company for this very reason.
- The ability to self-energize is a miraculous gift. You (and you alone) have the ability to refuel by spending time with yourself! There is no one else needed, and likewise, no one can stop or impede you.

Disadvantages of Being a Social Introvert:

- If social time and alone time are not properly balanced, social introverts, through compensation techniques can become high-functioning introverts, focusing on the needs of those around them at the expense of their own needs.
- Because Social Introverts appear less "quirky" and/or eccentric than other introverts, they are more often judged by society as moody, difficult and negative when they have become socially depleted.
- Social introverts are more likely to be challenged on their "introversion" because they blend into society easier.
- Social introverts will often be castigated by society as they become more adept at balancing their needs, i.e., "How come you

could run that meeting at work last week, but you can't come to my weekend house party because now you need "alone time"?!

- Social Introverts can be thwarted by last-minute changes or having a close friend cancel when they were needed as support in a highly charged social environment.

The Thinking Introvert: The Thinking Introvert is literally so deep in inward thought that the rest of the world can be roaring around them and they may have no idea what's going on. Thinking Introverts are quiet observers who can often be found lost in their own thoughts or daydreams. They will look at an idea or challenge from many different angles, figuring out solutions far more sophisticated than an extroverted thinkers. Thinking introverts are very often enormously creative and imaginative. They generally try and stay away from group projects or collaborations, because brainstorming with others annoys them. They prefer to figure out the entire picture by themselves, using their own unique but thorough thought processes. Whether they are dreamy idealists or highly methodical analysts, they are very deep souls, and their inspiration comes from within themselves, delving from their endless stores of long-term memory, rather than spouting out the first thing that comes to mind. Extroverted society may misinterpret their rich inner lives and deep concentration as a lack of practicality or intelligence, but nothing could be farther from the truth. Highly productive and successful musicians, authors, artists, and scientists fill the ranks of thinking introverts. They may communicate their complex theories better in writing rather than verbally, as getting their thoughts down on paper, allows them to be more detail oriented and thorough. Because they are so self-driven, thinking introverts may have to make if a point to touch base with loved ones and friends as well as mindfully make and keep appointments and dates for social activities. They are not resistant or anxious about social events; it oftentimes just doesn't even cross their busy, productive, thriving inner minds to stop, take a breath and interact with others!

Advantages of Being a Thinking Introvert:

- Thinking Introverts are the source of the world's innovators and visionaries. There is no change or forward movement without them!
- When left to their own devices, Thinking Introverts can single-handedly come up with complete, unique and elegant solutions to the world's problems and challenges.
- Thinking Introverts are masters at self-entertainment. They become immersed in movies, books, and games and can easily

imagine yourself actually taking part in the action.

- Because they are not averse to or anxious about social events, there is no problem attending them, as long as thinking introverts remember to go!
- Thinking Introverts are endlessly creative, imaginative and unique!

Disadvantages of Being a Thinking Introvert:

- People who don't know them may mistake their deep thinking and inner concentration for vapidness or stupidity.
- Insensitive, insecure people may ridicule the Thinking Introvert's ponderings and unique vision of the world, and naturally, this will hurt their feelings and make them feel self-conscious.
- They may be so deep in thought that they might forget to touch base with the rest of the world from time to time. This could result in mental stagnation and feelings of alienation.
- Thinking introverts may find it difficult to deal with day-to-day practicalities because they are so caught up in their rich inner life.
- They may sometimes feel out of step with the rest of the world and desire more people in their life who truly "get" them.

By Joshua Moore

The Anxious Introvert: One of the stereotypical hallmarks of being an introvert has always been that they are all shy. The Anxious Introvert is probably the reason this societal myth persists. Whether it is because they are "shy" or anxious, Anxious Introverts are often highly uncomfortable in social environments because they fear the unknown and are consumed by what other people think of them. Anxious Introverts negatively anticipate and project how painful the upcoming event will be, try to figure out any excuse to cancel attending, suffer through the actual event by shutting down or oversharing and then relive the event in an endless loop of self-loathing and shame, worrying about what everyone thought of what they perceive was their awkward behavior. Experiencing such a crippling cycle of anxiety and remorse, it is no wonder that Anxious Introverts avoid social gatherings at any cost. Sadly, it is not because they hate people or parties. They would love to enjoy the company of others at social gatherings but their unique set of coping mechanisms make this extremely difficult. Unfortunately, their suffering is not limited to the mental anguish described above. They are also plagued by physical symptoms including stomach and headaches, dizzy spells, trouble breathing and swallowing, insomnia, hot flashes and tunnel vision.

Probably the single biggest regret that Anxious Introverts have is that people have no idea who or what they are really like; what they are passionate about, what they are gifted at and what they are capable of. Like Thinking Introverts, often it is easier to express themselves through the written word rather than verbally. Through shear necessity, they are extremely detail-oriented and have the ability, through projection to see the big picture as well as to think out of the box. They can be extremely empathic, understanding only too well, the suffering and pain of others, and share the many gifts of the Empath (See my book, I am an Empath, to learn more).

The other good news for Anxious Introverts is that with behavioral therapy, medical intervention and alternative therapies such as mindfulness and meditation, they can temper and balance their anxiety without tampering with their ability to draw energy and inspiration from their introversion. Self-care and understanding will go a long way to allowing the Anxious Introvert to have a joyful, fulfilling life, empowered by their unique ability to self-fuel and appreciate the peace and quiet of solitude, enhanced by people and events enjoyed when and how they desire them.

Advantages of Being an Anxious Introvert:

- Anxious Introverts are great listeners and observers. They are often clued into subtle details that allow them to problem solve and finesse difficult situations.

- They have the ability to see through a "director's" lens, understanding the big picture and overarching goals.
- Anxious Introverts value true friendship and will be loyal allies through thick and thin.
- Because they are so guarded, Anxious Introverts have an air of mystery about them. Ironically, people are actually intrigued by the fact that they can't quite figure out what makes them tick!
- Their empathic and introverted tendencies enable them to appeal to a more diverse population, opening up global opportunities in cultures and societies that are less extroverted.

Disadvantages of Being an Anxious Introvert:

- Without self-care and balance, Anxious Introverts have the ability to literally make themselves ill.
- Anxious Introverts are often regarded by friends and employers as constantly "faking" illness or being hypochondriacs. This then is a negatively self-fulfilling cycle that society is judging them.
- Anxious Introverts can become exhausted by social events as well as by the anxiety they experience as they anticipate, endure and relive them.

- Their level of anxiety prevents them from "being in the moment" and makes them feel alienated.
- Anxious Introverts suffer from low self-esteem because they feel their avoidant behavior lets down others and eventually, themselves.

The Restrained Introvert: The Restrained or reserved Introvert may perhaps be the most misunderstood introvert of all. They are slow to act, slow to speak and slow to participate. It is this hesitancy that is misinterpreted time and time again. Restrained Introverts always make very sure that they have their facts straight, that they have something to add to the conversation, and most importantly, that it is worth it to them to divulge their thoughts or feelings. They are multi-layered people who take their time getting to know others and likewise, reveal their thoughts, feelings, and desires over time and with care that they are sharing themselves with kindred spirits. They are not shy. They are not in their own world. They are not anxious. They are good with who they are. This does not mean that they are immune to being misjudged or ridiculed for their reserved manner. They are capable of deep feelings and take great care that they don't misjudge the motives of others and allow themselves to become vulnerable or hurt. Restrained Introverts have an excellent sense of self, can be highly intelligent and once they warm to you, are funny, loving, loyal friends and life-partners. If they value and trust you, they will tell you exactly and thoroughly how they feel. If they don't; like as not they won't bother to interact. They are often misjudged by extroverts as cold, aloof, arrogant, misanthropic and difficult. These false judgments could not be further from the truth!

Advantages of Being a Restrained Introvert:

- Restrained Introverts are very sure within themselves of who they are. They are hard wired to be authentic and genuine. That is why they are slow to warm up to others – it is a self-preservation technique.
- They are thoughtful and accurate with their words and actions. Flippancy or the tendency to say the first thing that comes to mind is inconceivable to them!
- They are true experts in anything they care about. They put in the long hours and do the research and can be depended upon to have the correct answers.
- Restrained Introverts are dependable friends who will go above and beyond once you have earned their trust.
- They are not susceptible to gossip or slander, as they detest fakery of any sort and also are hypersensitive to being misjudged.

Disadvantages of Being a Restrained Introvert:

- Because of their low profile presence, Restrained Introverts may be overlooked or forgotten if they are not supported by more extroverted allies.
- Their physical and/or verbal slowness may be misinterpreted as dullness or disinterest.
- Restrained Introverts are slow to "market" themselves and may be less successful in a traditional interview or job settings.
- Their natural reserved personality may be misjudged as arrogance or coldness.
- The thoughtful, thorough way in which Restrained Introverts communicate may try the patience and attention span of less evolved individuals.

A Very Social Celebration of Introversion

I end this section with a personal reflection that I feel honored I was allowed to be a part of, and which I think beautifully illustrates the diversity and gifts of introversion when allowed to thrive in balance and acceptance.

Two years ago, I was invited to a destination wedding in the Adirondacks by my dear friends Becky and David. Becky is a classic Anxious Introvert who has a very successful marketing job and David is an amazing Restrained Introvert who is a historical enactor in Colonial

Williamsburg. They met, after mutual bumpy relationship roads, on Match.com and it was kismet. I have to say their personal introversions really are the yin to each other's yang. David, who has the intelligence and the insight to know what a rugged individual he is and who has forged a great career playing historical figures, offers the perfect support system to Becky, who suffers, despite her success, with new experiences and how society judges her. She has grown so much more confident since she has met and fallen in love with a fellow introvert who is absolutely comfortable in his skin. David, in turn, has become more outgoing to people he doesn't know because Becky has tempered his reserve and he feels he has less to lose, safe in the security of her love and loyalty!

Their wedding was a total celebration of introverted love. Unsurprisingly, more than a few of the friends and family are also diverse introverts, so the weekend was a virtual observation deck of introversion at its very best. Becky used her gift of being detail oriented to design and plan exactly how she wanted the venue to look, but she was also insightful enough to recognize that she would have to leave the implementation and coordination of the event to trusted allies so that she wouldn't become overwhelmed at the thirteenth hour. Fortunately, her friend Joe, a social introvert, was more than happy on the day of the event to step back from the social activities and become an ad hoc wedding coordinator, armed with lists and jobs for everyone from the caterers to the bartender to the sound guy. David's co-worker and good friend, April, an enchanting Thinking Introvert, spent the morning of the wedding making floral wreaths for the bridesmaids' hair and garlands for the outdoor chapel. There were no mandatory events, and people wandered in and out of the main farmhouse getting a cup of coffee or a bagel, chatting with the bridal party or sitting by the fireplace. David, knowing this event was a potential emotional flood zone, made sure there was time for walks in the woods, a trivial pursuit game with his college roommates and silly pictures with his groomsmen. Becky gave herself the gift of hours of unstructured time to enjoy being in the moment and to get ready at her leisure with help from her best friends. The only rule was that everyone needed to be at the outdoor chapel by 2 pm.

The wedding itself was a personal, touching ceremony, with beloved poems, songs from a gifted cousin and tears of joy and happiness. The reception consisted of an undemanding buffet and open house, with no socially mandated rituals but wonderful personalized touches, including a large scroll where people could take a moment and write their thoughts and reflections about the celebration. The bride and groom drifted in and out of the reception hall, as did the guests, who felt free to walk down to the lake or back to their cabins in the woods to rest and revive. Not only was it my personal favorite event of that year, but it was also the very first time I went to a wedding and absolutely believed I had witnessed an entire day devoted to two people without any other agenda. It was, in every sense of the phrase, Their Day.

It is my hope and my intention to utilize the second part of this book as a practical implementation guide to help you have more days, weeks, months and years that are designed and implemented to make the most of your introversion. Whether you are social, thinking, anxious, restrained or any combination of each, as an introvert you have the unique and innate power within you to draw and replenish energy that will allow you the potential to find balance and harmony in every aspect of your life. You need only to learn how to harness, utilize and focus this energy in sympathetic environments, surrounded by fellow introverts as well as extrovert allies in order to have the empowered relationships and personal and professional growth you have been searching for. I am excited by the prospect of unlocking this potential with you, and am so happy you have chosen to accompany me on this adventure!

Part Two

An Implementation Guide Designed to Unleash the Power of Introverts

It's one thing to read about the gifts and power of being an introvert. It's quite another to utilize these words and experience the freedom and power of living as a fully realized introvert in an extroverted society. My intention in writing the following guide is to differentiate between what it truly means to be an introvert and the social stereotypes including shyness and fear that have become associated with introversion. No one likes to be labeled in any manner that connotes being less able, and no one deserves to be disempowered in this way; summed up in one or two dismissive words. Introverts may be a minority in Western civilization, but there's a big old world out there, becoming more and more connected by technology and innovation, and it's high time that introverts are celebrated for their differences and respected for their powerful potential no matter where they live. With insight, preparation and practical advice, all introverts, regardless of whether they are social, thinking, anxious or restrained can learn to effectively communicate their hopes, dreams, and desires and see them through to successful materialization, without having to change who they are. Rather who they are should only empower and benefit their personal and professional growth and endeavors!

Taking the Fear Factor Out of Being Introverted

When approached to write this book, my publishers, readers and clients asked me to focus on helping introverts overcome specific fears associated with being introverted, ranging from talking on the telephone, riding on an elevator and making small talk to public speaking, forming relationships and self-promotion for professional growth. I welcomed this challenge but felt I must first dispel the myth that being introverted makes people more fearful. Fear is an equal opportunist. It does not prey only on the introverted! There are plenty of extroverts out there with as many or more fears as introverts. Society, and perhaps even introverts themselves have promoted the assumption that being introverted means being fearful.

Here are several universal truths about fear:

- Fear always represents something in your life that needs to be identified, addressed and resolved
- Fear is often an excuse for something we don't want to deal with, something we are in denial about, something we are trying

to avoid because we dislike it or it makes us uncomfortable.

- Resolving Fear often unlocks Opportunity for Growth and Power.

Let's now apply these universal truths to the general state of being introverted. Should someone who gathers their energy and inspiration from within be more susceptible to fear? It would seem to me, that the power to resolve issues from within could be a formidable weapon in the battle to overcome fear. Could someone who was introverted use fear as an excuse to avoid resolving their issues about social events, being over stimulated and controlling their energy output? Hmmm...I think they might. What might happen if an introvert resolved certain issues they had that hindered the quality of their life, without changing who they were as individuals? That sounds a lot like personal and professional growth to me!

I don't mean to make light of fear. Fear is real, and it is crippling at the moment it is being experienced. The distinction I am making, however, is that fear can be and is experienced by both introverts and extroverts, and, actually, introverts have a few innate abilities and coping strategies to help them resolve fear BETTER than extroverts:

- The ability to think before speaking or acting – Extroverts tend to blurt out what they are feeling or thinking without a plan because they need outside input in order to make a plan. As long as Introverts ACT upon their fully envisioned plans, they have the edge when it comes to resolving fear based issues.

- The ability to see The Big Picture – because Introverts are by necessity such great observers and listeners of what is going on around them, they tend to have a much more panoramic overview of situations that could cause fear. This enables them to pinpoint specific pitfalls or challenges and also allows them to plan how to deal with them. Extroverts are too busy gathering external energy and feedback and tend to focus only on how they are feeling at the moment; while sometimes lacking the ability to even distinguish what is the source of their fear.

- The ability to prioritize which fears need to be addressed and resolved as life-hindering, and which fears can be tempered by avoidance and alternate routes – once again, introverts have the edge when it comes 1. To knowing themselves well and 2. To recognizing precisely which "fears" are compromising their happiness and growth potential as opposed to social challenges that are merely an annoyance or frustration. Extroverts, because of their visceral need for external stimulus often have to plunge forward no matter the depth of discomfort, in order to satisfy their energetic needs.

I would like to expand upon the last bullet as I think the gift of fear prioritization offers a practical and concrete solution to many fear-based issues.

Please take a moment or two and write a list including every fear you currently have. No fear is too trivial for this list. Now make two lists from your original – one comprised of fears that don't hinder your growth potential or true happiness and one comprised of the fears that do. At this point, before you begin to plan either your avoidance or resolution strategies, you need to factor in your introvert type and how it will affect your strategies. Finally, you need to prioritize the fears of both lists, so you can figure out which ones need to be addressed first in order to immediately improve the quality of your happiness and growth potential.

I have included a short example of what I want you to do:

Complete List of Fears:
- Talking on the telephone
- Asking for and getting a promotion at work
- Making introductions
- Small talk
- Using public restrooms
- Asking people out for a date
- Ordering at a restaurant

- Getting on an elevator

Now make two lists:

Fears That Hinder my Growth and Happiness
- Asking for and getting a promotion at work
- Asking out people for a date
- Using public restrooms
- Ordering at a Restaurant

Fears That are Annoying or Frustrating
- Talking on the telephone
- Making introductions
- Small talk
- Getting on an elevator

Factor in Your Introversion Type:

Social: Although you are probably more than capable of resolving most of these fears, you will have to pay special attention to your finite stores of social energy, and use careful scheduling as well as balanced time-away to accomplish your goals.

Thinking: You need to always factor in your creativity and imagination when strategizing your fear resolutions. It is also incredibly important that you give yourself as much thinking time as you need and to protect yourself from the reactions of others.

Anxious: You need to discern if your fears are introversion-based or social anxiety-based. If they are social anxiety based, you need (and can!) identify and resolve the anxiety through therapy, medication or alternative therapies. You need to learn to protect yourself from the judgment of others whether it is real or assumed.

Restrained: You need to decide if the issue is important enough for you to resolve. You also need to consider how your words and actions affect others, as this may be the source of your fears! You may find that you have relatively few fears and many more frustrations and annoyances that are hindering your quality of life.

Prioritize:

Number one fear that hinders my growth and happiness

- Asking out people on a date

Number one fear that annoys or frustrates me

- Talking on the telephone

Now let's play out what resolving these two fears might look like...

How to talk on the phone fear free:

- Isolate your fear – What exactly are you afraid of? Having to make small talk and not have a visual reference? Using up precious social energy? Not being able to keep your focus? Being judged by the person on the other end of the line? Taking too long to answer their questions? Figure out exactly what you fear so you can strategize solutions and resolutions.

- Once you know exactly what you fear about phone talk, come up with specific strategies to prevent the fearful thing from happening: Write down your main talking points and after identifying yourself, get right to the point. Schedule phone work for a time when you feel full of social-energy, and plan alone time immediately after. Script your phone call before making it and use phone time as needed to acquire face to face time in person, online or through an email or letter that will allow you to fully describe your reason for the communication. Envision the person at the other end of the line as a sympathetic presence who needs the information you are going to impart. If you need more time to formulate your answers, simply state that you need to figure things out before you give an answer and will get back to them as soon as possible.

- Do your research: Find books, articles, blogs and community discussions online that offer tips and advice on this specific fear. Remember, as silly as it may make you feel that you fear the phone, it is an extremely common problem for introverts! I'm personally always so gratified and amazed when I come upon a fellow sufferer to whatever problem I'm having who's figured out a solution that resonates with me.

- Practice, practice, practice. Take a moment to review after each phone call you make. Jot down what went well and what didn't. Take some alone-time and envision the ideal phone call and how you can make that happen on a regular basis.
- Minimize phone calls to a specific time of the day or, if possible keep them to an absolute minimum. I have introverted friends who are on the phone from the time they arrive at work until the time they leave, but on their own time have a strict "no-phone" policy. We are so fortunate to live in the world of online technology where texting, emailing, messengering, skyping, WhatsApp, and join.me can substitute and many times replace a phone call!

How to fearlessly ask someone out on a date:

- Isolate your fear – what exactly are you afraid of? Getting through the introductions and surface chat that you know from experience drains you of precious energy and shuts you down? Not being able to verbally communicate your desire to get to know this person better? Feeling mortified at the possibility that your advances will be rebuffed or ridiculed? Concerned that you'll come off as cold or inapproachable? Worried that you'll reveal too much of yourself and become vulnerable on some level? It might be difficult, but when it comes to fears that arrest your potential to form relationships, you need to face what you fear most head on so that you can tackle the problem accurately. When the exact source of fear is unknown, it is impossible to resolve it.

- Strategize – once you've isolated the specific cause of your fear, brainstorm ways in which you can overcome your discomfort. Make a list of all the reasons having a relationship is such a priority for you. Make another list of exactly what qualities you are looking for in a potential date. Ask close, trusted friends to include you in small groups of mutual friends as well as like-minded strangers and give yourself warm up time through activities such as board games, cooking, watching movies or hiking. Remember you are an expert observer and listener. Once you have positioned yourself in a low-pressure social situation, sit back and take in the people around you. Join the conversation when you have something to contribute but let other, extroverted types take the lead in keeping the party going. Focus on staying in the moment, so if someone seeks you out, you are "available" to interact. Bring your authenticity with you. Don't exhaust yourself trying to be someone you are not, especially when you are trying to find someone to date! The whole point of this challenging exercise is to find a kindred spirit you can be your introverted self with.

- Do Your Research -- Find books, articles, blogs and community discussions online that offer tips and advice on dating and relationships. Don't limit your scope to advice and help specifically for introverts or for that matter, even dating. My writer partner Helen Glasgow and I have written two books that are great alternative resources for relationship challenges. **The Emotional Intelligence Spectrum** focuses on growth and change through the lens of balance and intrapersonal intelligence and their positive impact on relational disturbances and challenges. Our **Growth Mindset** book (can be found for free in the beginning of this book) tackles the challenges of relationships through two very different personal and professional viewpoints that offer theoretical and concrete advice for personal and professional growth including finding your tribe, your co-pilots, and trusted collaborators. As I said earlier, you never know what is going to personally resonate for you, but when you find it, you will know it, and it will help!
- Actions speak louder than words – Once you have thoroughly researched and strategized, you must put your theories

and thoughts to the test. Walking the talk of the dating game is a difficult challenge for any introvert, but there will be no change without action. It is important to remember that this is a work in progress, and introverts are fortunate in that they are experts at personal reflection, so if an early attempt at dating is less than successful they are more than up to the job of taking some time to figure out where improvements could be made for the next venture. And again, that next venture must occur! Dating and relationships are so important to the health and happiness of the introvert who cannot, despite their fondness for looking inward and solitary reflection and rejuvenation, exist in an ideal state without human interaction. I know I'm preaching to the choir, or in this instance, perhaps the soloist but I would be remiss if I didn't reinforce the necessity of a relational support system in the lives of every introvert.

- Modern technology is your ally and quite possibly your match.com-maker! If initial face-to-face contact fills you with dating dread, please look into online dating services. They seem almost to have been designed specifically for the single introvert looking for prospective dates. The combination of a highly formulated survey, which if filled out thoughtfully and completely, should match you with like-minded people, coupled with the opportunity to express your individual likes and dislikes in a descriptive introduction, offers introverts of all types the comfort of the written word, composed in their own time frame, with the ability to edit and refine to their detail-oriented heart's content. Also, the ability to review responses, make a solitary decision whether to proceed to the next step or not, as well as the transitional scheme of chatting online before actually meeting up face to face, gives introverts multiple opportunities to put themselves at ease and warm up to the prospect of a traditional date. I personally feel that society has given online dating sites a bad rep. I think online dating is a great example of getting what you give, in that, if you let it support you as you search for an authentic relationship with your best intentions in mind, you will most likely reap what you sow.

You may be surprised that the process for quality of life hindering fears and annoying/frustrating fears are quite similar. The reason for this is how introverts process challenges and the gifts they possess that will help them overcome them. Really the only difference between the two types of fear is the degree in which they affect your happiness and ability to grow and succeed in life. When fear is merely annoying like small talk or avoidable like riding roller coasters, it's quite easy to plan alternative routes around them or avoid them all together. When a fear hinders your happiness and growth potential, it needs to be positively identified, strategized and tempered or eradicated from your life path. And everyone's priority of fear is unique to their particular life path. Small talk and rollercoasters probably won't have much of an impact on most of our lives, but if you are an introvert born into an amusement park empire and your existence depends on chatting to adrenaline junkies...well then, you need to face your fears, schedule regular visits to a silent monastery, take your Dramamine and jump onto that Tilt-a-Whirl of life!

Introverted Care: Protecting yourself in an Extroverted Society

When I came up with the title for this portion of the implementation guide I originally used the term introverted 'self-care,' but upon seeing it in print, I was struck by the redundancy of those three words...inward-turning self-care! However, it also made me think about impact of those words and I came to the realization, that once again, the very essence of introversion contains elements of self-preservation, if we take heed of them and respect those who are introverts as gifted, unique individuals rather than odd, shy people who really need to stop being afraid of everything, get out of their "comfort zone" and assimilate themselves into "normal" society. I wish the preceding sentence were a gross exaggeration of how many in western civilization view introverts, but sadly it is not the case. Therein lies the necessity of a section devoted to the self-protection of introverts.

I threw quotation marks around the term "comfort zone" and if you've read my book the Growth Project you know why. It is possibly my most hated psychological phrase. At the risk of repeating myself, I can't understand why any coach, therapist, healer or spiritual advisor would ever refer to the place or state of mind an unhappy, discontented person has been existing in as their "comfort zone"! As far as I'm concerned, "comfort zone" should refer to the future ideal destination of someone in the throes of personal and/or professional growth, be they introverts, extroverts or any combination of the two! And as to the word "normal", well all I can say to that misnomer is a classic, adolescent WHATEVER!!!

When researching this book, apart from using my own work with introverts as clients, I read many, many book, articles, posts and blogs by and about introverts and the daily challenges they face in an extrovert-centric society. Out of all those writings, there was only one entry that suggested advice on how to make introverts feel more comfortable in the workplace...one! This just strengthened my intention to give some practical concrete advice on how introverts can and should protect themselves; at work, and at home.

A self-protection primer for the workplace

The workplace of the new millennium has, in general, become a much more competitive, benefit-barren, production-oriented environment as companies have become more streamlined and workers have adjusted to being more flexible and less valued. Gone are the glory days when prospective employers seduced employees with signing bonuses, free health insurance, anger management courses for explosive executives (I swear, I worked for one!) and on-site childcare facilities. Self-care has become the buzzword for employee services, and no-one should heed the call more than introverts. Workplaces are generally set up for extroverts to excel in. It is much more time and cost efficient to cater to team spirit and the greater good than to customize the work environment to the gifts and comfort of an introvert who thrives in a smaller group setting or even, dare I say, a private office! Introverts need to learn to insulate themselves from the overstimulation of open office plans, large group meetings, free for all brainstorming sessions and presentations where public speaking is rewarded, and the squeaky wheels of competitive and aggressive self-marketing receive the grease of promotion and monetary compensation. And yet, introvert or not, whether social, thinking anxious or restrained, for the majority, work we must.

Here are ten practical, non-invasive, transparent strategies that will not only give introverts protection in the workplace but allow them to flourish and thrive.

- Learn to take credit for your work: There is nothing worse for anyone, in a work environment than consistently going above and beyond, but getting no recognition for doing it, or worse still, having someone else hijack your success and claim it as their own. In the recent film, Hidden Figures, one of the lead characters, a brilliant female mathematician working in the backroom of NASA keeps signing her work, to the increasing anger of her male superior. Despite his resentment and professional jealousy, she persists, and finally, she begins to receive the acknowledgment she so richly deserves. No matter how private and unassuming you wish to be, you must find a way to take credit for your work. It is essential to your professional career path, and your personal self-esteem. If you need motivation simply understand that the more you are known for what you excel at in the workplace, the more time and monetary compensation you will be given to perform those specific tasks, and the less time you will have to spend painfully perform tasks that drain you of your social energy, make you feel unbalanced and rob you of your self-confidence.

- Identify fellow introverts in your place of business: Use your gift of observation and figure out who else is an introvert, as well as what type of introvert they seem to be. Find ways to bond with each other and form a collaboration, where you share advice, news, ideas, and ways to help each other survive.

- Seek out Extrovert Allies: Just as you don't want anyone making stereotypical assumptions about you, I know you would never make assumptions about all extroverts! Remember, there is some truth in all generalities and in some cases opposites do attract. Do your research and reach out to extroverts who seem receptive to your efforts. As you get to know them, ask their advice on how to get along easier in the workplace, and in turn, help them when they are in need of self-reflection and insight into the big picture!

- Learn to speak up in meetings: Prepare yourself by asking for agendas before the meeting, so you have time to reflect and prepare. Start small, and make it your intention to speak once, on a point you are an expert on. Understand the power of speaking selectively and only on the occasion when you have something innovative or inspirational to add, and you will go far. People stop listening to those who speak all the time. As Shakespeare said, it's "all sound and fury, signifying nothing."

- Seek out opportunities to showcase your gifts: if you wait around to be assigned that dream project that you excel at, chances are you'll end up standing around in the same place for a very long time, not knowing what to do with your arms and hands. Push beyond "cog in the wheel" work mentality and proactively create opportunities to show off your skills. Volunteer to work on a special presentation if it requires the skill set you shine at. Keep your well-trained ears to the ground and offer to troubleshoot when a co-worker is having difficulties meeting a deadline. None of these activities require you to be aggressive or to do anything you aren't great at, to begin with. The extra benefit you will reap will be increased exposure in the workplace, as a helpful, kind person and a gifted employee. Win.win.

- Hate the Spotlight? Position yourself as the guy/gal behind every great leader: When you go to a hit Broadway show, chances are you won't walk away knowing the name of the lighting designer or the person responsible for constructing the wigs, but guess what? They are talented, fulfilled artists, more than happy to work backstage, enjoy a great reputation in the industry, and make a ton of money doing what they love. Transfer that position to your workplace. Align yourself with an experienced leader or help a talented newcomer up the corporate ladder. If you work with the right people, your professional value will soar, and you will be monetarily compensated for doing what you love in the privacy you crave.

- Find safe harbors during professional development days, seminars and conferences: Nothing puts the fear in an introvert's heart more than a day of interactive professional development! Arm yourself with an emergency toolkit for these trying times. Volunteer to run the PowerPoint, set up the room, act as whiteboard scribe, narrate events with a prewritten script, coordinate groups and all the other helpful chores extroverts loathe and introverts grasp at like a life preserver in a stormy sea. If you have to actively participate, align yourself with those introverts and extrovert allies you identified earlier. There is strength in numbers!

- Prepare for Presentations: if your job requires that you do a presentation, make sure you give yourself lots of that scheduled downtime to completely envision every last detail, including what potential questions might come up and how you will answer them. Do not even think about winging one bit of this! If you aren't already an anxious introvert, this type of Night at the Improv stunt will transform you into one. Practice in front of trusted friends and loved ones if you feel a dry run will ease your nerves. If it's good enough for professional politicians before a national debate, it's good enough for you.

- Become the expert on cutting edge technology: As I've mentioned before, today's technology is often an introvert's best friend. Stay up on the latest social media trends, as well as any proprietary programs your workplace might be utilizing. You could very well end up training your department and getting paid for it. Also, more and more marketing departments are hiring their own in-house online media specialists.

- Use breaks, lunches, fire drills and restrooms as mobile charging stations: In other words, any time you are left to your own devices, scheduled or unscheduled, spend it alone, replenishing your energy. And if someone questions your solitude, simply explain your needs as an introvert, or better yet, let them borrow this book!

With a Family Like This, Who Needs Extroverts?

Growing up, I guess you could say we lived in an Introvert's paradise. Our home was a rambling old former boarding house with plenty of space for all of us to go off on our own. My mother was an Anxious Introvert who loved to read and watch her "soaps." My brother was a Restrained Introvert, often found holed up in his room creating massive soft sculptures he'd hang from the ceiling light fixture. I was a Thinking Introvert, and I had my own music room where I taught myself to play piano and would sight-read classic movie scores I borrowed from the library, for hours on end. My Dad was a charming Social Introvert who would sing and dance through his days as the local music teacher and then retire to his nest where he would read Thoreau and listen to jazz. My poor little sister was the lone extrovert, and she would flit from one to another of us until we swatted her away like a gnat, with our books or newspapers. It was an eccentric household, but it worked for us.

What happens though when one's family isn't quite so like-minded? If this were a book about extroverts, I would have interviewed my sister for this segment, but it isn't so I won't.

How does an introverted Mom cope with an extroverted toddler? What can the adult introvert child of an extrovert family do to cope when visiting during the holidays? How does an introverted young bride survive the first visit to her raucous extroverted in-laws? How does an introverted young adult who has been enabled by a doting father prepare for college life? What's the dynamic and where's the balance in a mixed extrovert/introvert multi-generational family?

Here are ten more "family friendly" strategies and techniques designed to protect introverts from...their loved ones!

- Create and stick to strict routines – If you are an introvert who has given birth to an extroverted child, keep them as active as you can stand, allowing them to socialize with other extroverts, participating in playgroups and going to the local park. Oddly, their happiness at being with others will allow you to be calmer, especially if you find activities that are more focused on participating with the child, so there isn't a lot of time for the moms and dads to chat, i.e., music classes and parent/baby yoga rather than playgroups where the parents stand around and socialize. Basically, wear your extrovert out, stick to consistent routines and you will be rewarded with solid nap times and night sleeps that give you precious time to decompress and re-energize. The unbreakable rule is when a child is sleeping you are taking care of yourself! Also, take advantage of weekends and vacations when a working partner can step up, as well as Grandparents, Aunties, and dear friends. Instead of date nights, schedule weekly downtimes. If you both work, devote the first hour or two at home to your extroverted child, so that their socializing, bonding needs are met, and stick to consistent bed routines and times, so there will be precious time left for you to relax.

- Dare to stay at a hotel – If you are an adult child coming home for the holidays to a family home full of extroverts, the experience of spending intense, lengthy times with them can be jarring and exhausting. Come up with a good reason, i.e., you don't think Mom should have to spend her holidays cleaning up after you, you want to make sure there's room for all your brother's kids, etc., and announce ahead of time, so no one is surprised that you have booked into the local b and b. Knowing that a quiet single room awaits you at the end of each day should go a long way in getting you through crazy, chaotic family times!

- Adjust your schedule to take advantage of extroverted awake and sleep patterns – If you've recently married into an extroverted tribe, are visiting for the first time and can't swing the hotel tip listed above, observe their social patterns, and when they are thoroughly involved with each other, slip away and get an early night's sleep. Wake early, while they are all sleeping in and go for a walk, to prepare you for the festivities ahead. Also, endear yourself to them by volunteering to run errands, walk the dog, pick up kids, or grocery shop and use the solo car and errand time as a mini-recharge.

- Don't allow family members to enable you – It's one thing for your extrovert family to understand and respect that you are an introvert – they are your first extrovert allies, modeling positive and supportive behavior that you can be on the lookout to replicate throughout your life. It's another thing when extrovert parents and siblings enable you, allowing you to duck out of life's opportunities, and develop fears and avoidance issues. Well-meaning relatives can often end up treating an introverted family member like there is something wrong with them, perpetuating the stereotype that introverts are odd, unsociable, awkward people. Don't fall into the pit. If you can't verbalize your feelings, write down your thoughts and share them with family members whose "unconditional love" is stifling your very existence.

- Take a family inventory and live and let live – If you want your family to understand and respect your introverted needs, you need to do them the courtesy of understanding and respecting their individual needs as well. Instead of wasting your energy deflecting and avoiding theirs's, take some time to observe each of them, analyzing each of their levels and types of extroversion and introversion. Discuss your findings, one-on-one and ask family members what they like and dislike about the group dynamic. This is a great opportunity for the type of in-depth, meaningful dialogue you crave and everyone, no matter their temperament, appreciates the chance to be genuinely heard.

- Be a mentor to younger introverted siblings – If you have younger brothers and sisters who are struggling with being introverted, take them under your wing and show them the ropes. You will gain a loyal friend for life, and they will gain the strength and confidence to celebrate their introversion. Mentoring is a very gratifying, empowering experience and it shouldn't be an extroverts-only activity. You may discover hidden leadership qualities you never knew you possessed.

- Enlighten older relatives – along with being extrovert-centric, Western society hasn't always been at the forefront of understanding people's differences and some outdated theories on how to get people to fit in by forcing them to change or bullying them have been cruel and harsh. It's important to understand, however, that older people believed that in doing these things, they were helping their loved ones. Talk with older relatives in a non-confrontational manner about introversion and what we now understand, and you may not only teach an elder new information but also heal a hidden introvert and make them feel very differently about themselves.

- If you can't teach or reach 'em, avoid 'em – Unfortunately, there will always be people, because of fear or ignorance who will refuse to change how they feel and act towards others they have labeled "different." Some of them may be members of your family. If you've done your best to enlighten them and they still ridicule you and make you feel bad, you need to stop interacting with them. You've done everything you can, and unless they are willing to change, there will be no further resolution.

- Control your home environment when relatives come to stay: If you have an extended family, sooner or later it's going to be your turn to host. If extroverts are part of the mix prepare for them. Have age-appropriate jobs or projects all set up for them to accomplish throughout their visit so you can get back to your routine. I have a friend whose Dad recently remarried an extreme extrovert. My friend bravely asked this woman's son, who seemed relatively quiet and reserved, how he put up with her when she visited and he proceeded to show my friend a laundry list of minor home improvements his mom had accomplished for them over the years. The next time Dad and his energetic bride came to visit, my friend had stations set up with all sorts of "honey-do" chores she needed to be done. Dad and stepmom thoroughly enjoyed themselves and my friend was rewarded with a new and improved home and much warmer feelings towards her Dad's new wife!

- Tell people what you need before you run out of gas – Instead of white-knuckling it through a family event until you suddenly shut down and run away with no explanation, leaving the family who is offended or hurt by your abrupt behavior. Pre-empt this negative situation by clearly stating your needs in advance of the event. Call up and say that you may very well have to leave the event early or arrive a bit later than the start time, to give yourself wiggle room. Expressing that your need for time to yourself is a necessity rather than a choice can sometimes clear the air. Often by simply communicating what you need, you can spare yourself a lot of family drama.

The need to protect yourself whether at work or home is of prime importance. The introvert's unique inward source of energy replenishment relies on it, and his/her self-esteem, feelings and rights as a human being demands it. There are lots of different people in this world who need to protect themselves and it's never because they are weak or fragile. It is because the unique gifts they were born with make them sensitive to the energy of others and vulnerable to people who are capable of literally draining them. My book **I am an Empath** explores self-protection for people who are highly attuned to the feelings and needs of others. It will offer you more self-protection advice and, if your heightened ability to observe others includes feeling their pain to a high degree, may help you in your quest to conserve your social energy and preserve who you are.

By Joshua Moore

The Balancing Act of the Happy Introvert

Once you have started to conquer your introverted "fears" and learned to protect yourself at work and home, you should be in a much better place to focus on finding and maintaining balance in your life. In **The Emotional Intelligence Spectrum**, we discuss the goal of reaching and maintaining a state of Emotional Enlightenment, which requires a careful balance of happiness and endless opportunities for continued personal and professional growth. The necessity for creating this state of balance is because being permanently happy is not a realistic or sustainable goal. True happiness predicates the ability to appreciate where you are at the moment but also being able to anticipate future opportunities to enjoy the success and satisfaction of identifying, striving towards and attaining new growth goals. So once you have reached your safe place or what I like to think of as your TRUE "comfort zone" of introversion, you are now ready to work on balance.

What does balance look like for the introvert? Again, we must refer to the specific introvert type to help formulate the complete answer to this question, but generally, introverted balance depends on the ability to maintain consistent energy-replenishing solitude while carving out periods of our lives dedicated to interacting with sympathetic friends and allies as well as "strangers", as all of these groups will offer us opportunities to grow both personally and professionally.

Dealing with Strangers

I'm starting with strangers because they are the most challenging interaction most introverts can envision and because until you are skilled at dealing with strangers, you cannot expect to transition into making friends or allies out of them. And that's what strangers have the potential to be: Friends and allies.

Fear of Strangers is not going to be one of those frustrating or annoying fears we can try to avoid. It belongs at the top of many introvert's Fears That Hinder Growth and Happiness. Perhaps it already made your list earlier in this book. Look at it this way: every time you avoid interacting with a stranger you are missing the opportunity for personal and/or professional growth as well as the opportunity for a potential friendship or a positive alliance. I am going to deconstruct the process of interacting with a stranger in the following steps:

IMPORTANT NOTE: For the purposes of this concrete stranger interaction technique, I need to first make a very important distinction. When I write about interacting with strangers, I mean necessary interactions. i.e. a job interview, networking, meeting your children's teachers, a first date, even sitting with your best friend's co-workers at her wedding reception. I'm not talking about dealing with random strangers on a bus or airplane or the stranger that bumps into your grocery cart while you are standing in line at the supermarket. While these stranger interactions can feel just as traumatizing at the moment, they can be avoided or intercepted and certainly deflected by a polite but busy attitude, a nod or wave and a sudden change of direction, iPod, cell phones, books or the urgent need to clean and organize a messy brief case or purse. All joking aside, you have every right to politely deflect unwanted attention from a stranger. I refuse to tell you that you have to become good at small talk and "fake it till you make it" Bad advice like that is what motivated me to write this book!

How to Interact with Strangers who could Impact your Growth or Happiness

- If possible, give yourself sufficient alone time to prepare and consider outcomes.
- If possible, prepare yourself with thoughts of a positive outcome. This is the opposite of negative self-fulfilling prophecies, and is just as effective but in a good way!
- Take a deep breath and stand tall (this will actually give your body a physiological signal and will release hormones to make you more prepared and alert)
- Make eye contact briefly but surely and smile. This isn't a contest or a stand down

like the handshake of the current American President. This is just body language signaling confidence and openness.

- Make an initial opening statement that you have thought about beforehand (ex: appropriate greeting for a job interview; networking situation; meeting your child's teacher, etc.) This is the extent of your small talk duties, and technically you are no longer strangers.

- Use your love of genuine, meaningful dialogue, cut to the chase and start talking about what's important to you about this meeting, using the environment you are in, the importance of the event, what you love or hate about it, or why you are here. If it's an interview situation, follow protocol and wait to respond to questions which you should approach as helpful cues rather than tricks to trip you up.

- Stay in the moment, and observe the person you are interacting with as well as actively listening to what they are saying. Don't self-edit or mentally beat yourself up. Listen and observe so you can reflect back what they are trying to communicate to you authentically.

- If you feel the person, you are interacting with is warming to you, relax and be honest about your nerves or initial concerns with this meeting.

- If you feel the person you are interacting with is not warming to you, consider that they may be a less enlightened introvert than you are, and may be running low or about to shut down because of their energy depletion.

- Know when to leave. Don't belabor or draw out your goodbyes. You, as an introvert are an expert on judging when things are coming to a rapid close. Use your best intuition and wrap it up! You only have a finite amount of energy, and you are more than likely due to a serious break at this point.

Making Friends

It makes sense if as an introvert, you need and desire lots of time alone, that your very environment of choice might end up hindering your ability to make friends. However, just because you enjoy being alone, doesn't mean that you will never end up feeling lonely. Our society has a hard time differentiating between being alone and being lonely. Being alone, whether by choice or fortune, is a physical state of being. Being lonely is an emotional state of being. One doesn't eliminate or, for that matter, guarantee the other. In the same manner, being an introvert, regardless of specific type, doesn't eliminate the desire for friendship or guarantee that you won't have friends, **no matter how anyone else reacts to or judges your introversion** (the last part of this sentences is especially important for Anxious Introverts).

When making friends, it is very important for introverts to keep in mind what activities they enjoy participating in, where they enjoy going out, and how often they can realistically tolerate socializing. The answers to these questions will offer excellent clues as to the type of people they should be trying to be friends with. This friendship making concept may be quite a wake-up call to introverts who have been lead to believe they need to make friends with popular, extremely social people even though these extroverted types may be the very source of their friendship phobia! Instead of forcing yourself to interact with people who society has labeled "fun" and "popular", the introvert needs to respect his/her personal boundaries and choose friends who will enhance an introverted lifestyle. When you planfully design the way you want your social life to look, there is way more potential that you will find and attract like-minded people, be they introverts or extroverts, who you have much more in common with.

5 Basic Things to Remember When Making Friends

- Who You Are: Don't lose yourself in your search for friendship. Your authentic and unique self is your best selling point, and remembering who you are will also remind you of who you want to spend time with.

- Translate your Thoughts to Action: Once you have figured out who you are looking for it is time to stop thinking and start actively seeking them out. The process you use to dispel "fears" will serve you well here!

- Technology is your friend! If talking on the phone is your enemy, use texting, email, and social media to make that initial contact.

- Follow Up: Introverts are notorious for not following up when people make contact. Answer the phone message, email, text or note! This is what you've been waiting for. Don't let your fear of energy depletion or overcommitting conquer you!

- Don't Psych Yourself Out: If your initial attempts aren't responded to immediately, give it some time. Consider the possibility that your new friend might be...introverted!

Specific Friendship Tips for Specific Introvert Types:

Social Introverts:

- Be mindful of your energy levels when actively making friends. Depleting your energy makes you appear moody or as if you aren't having fun, so your social energy gas tank needs to be full, especially in the early days when people are getting to know you.

Thinking Introverts:

- It is especially important for you to make friends who share and/or respect your creativity and imagination. If a friend starts teasing you or belittling you about your work or your intense inner life, they are not a true friend! You do not have to put up with passive or aggressive bullies as a trade-off for companionship.

Anxious Introverts:

- Learn how to express your fears and anxiety upfront. For you, transparency is essential as it will explain why you act the way you act as well as weed out people who can't or won't understand your issues. A friend is someone who cares enough to care!

Restrained Introverts:

- Be mindful that your natural reticence and the extra time you need to warm up to people may be misinterpreted as coldness or abruptness and if you can, temper this with humor or diligence. On the other hand, trust your innate ability to know if someone is worth opening up yourself to.

The Need for Trusted Allies

What are allies? Allies are all the people in your life who offer you support and have your back. You can rely on them for advice, inspiration, help, and protection. If introverts are so self-sufficient why do they need allies? Introverts need allies to help them conserve their energy, to protect their specific vulnerabilities and to act as an envoy and help communicate their gifts and abilities to an extrovert-centric society. When looking for allies either in your professional or personal life, you are not always looking for the same qualities you would be seeking in friendship. Natural allies may very well have the same qualities as a friend, but unexpected allies, (including extroverts) will possess skill sets you don't have, but that will complement and enhance yours. Just like friendship, successful alliances are built on an equal give and take, i.e., you both need to bring something to the party. You also need to respect each other, as well as your differences to form and maintain a successful alliance.

Potential Allies:

- Your Boss: Your superior at work can become a powerful ally, supporting your work, protecting you from other employees and championing your talents and gifts. It is important that you communicate through words and actions your efficacy and productivity in the workplace, show loyalty (an introvert specialty!) and be transparent when issues connected to your introversion threaten your ability to perform your job.

- Support Staff: As an introvert with limited energy to interact with others, support staff can end up being your knights in shining armor! There is a reason the word "support" is part of their title. Whether they are IT people, secretarial staff, finance specialists or traffic managers, get to know them, and they will ease many potentially frustrating situations throughout your work day. Show them respect, acknowledge them and thank them for their efforts and they will be loyal allies.

- Long Term Employees: People who have spent their entire career in one place become experts in how the business runs. They've seen it all including good and bad changes, staff increases and cuts and the gamut of professional triumphs, as well as spectacular personnel, fails. Let them talk, and do your best active listening as they regale you with cautionary tales about employees with an agenda, and departments with a vendetta as well as who the good guys are. Keep their confidence and respect their knowledge and you will have an invaluable ally and avoid energy-depleting messes.

- Professional or Personal Interest Group Members: Your job or your personal interests and hobbies may require or motivate you to be a member of a special interest group. Be it the local chamber of commerce, a union, a long distance running club or a local charity, you will always have the mission of the group in common and can use this to find natural and unexpected allies to work with in this specific environment. This will also help you be more productive and effective within the group, as you will have formed a collaboration and added another, possibly more extroverted voice to reach your common goals. Through these types of collaborative alliances, you may also discover hidden leadership talents you never knew you possessed. True story: I knew an introvert who became involved in the process of unionizing his workplace and ended up representing the employees at the meetings, because of his quiet passion for worker's rights and his years of on the job experience. The support and earned the respect of his fellow workers allowed him to find the strength and energy to lead.

- Advisors, Life Coaches, Therapists, etc.: There is an entire subset of "allies for hire" that are attractive alternatives to introverts of all types. For a mutually agreed upon fee, they are there to support and advise you as experts in their field, and all you have to do is to find a way to communicate your needs. As a matter of fact, if they are good at what they do, these professional allies can even help you do that!

- Neighbors: Neighbors are an interesting potential source of allies. They're kind of a community-based hybrid. Not necessarily anyone you might be friends with, you may still end up being a touchstone for one another throughout the years, because of your common interest in adjacent properties and the welfare of the neighborhood. It's always wise to try and develop an "over the fence" relationship that respects boundaries but enables as needed collaboration when the occasion presents itself.

- Family: Family members are probably the original source for allies. Be it an older brother, a "sister-cousin" or a favorite Uncle, often we are the fortunate recipients, through our birthright, of a built in an unconditional ally. These are the relatives we've literally known forever, who "get us" in a way no one else ever will. They are our sounding boards and the source of honest but loving feedback. If you are lucky enough to have an alliance like this, please use them to work on your specific introversion issues, but always check in with them to make sure they are not becoming burned out or fatigued by your needs. They will probably never tell you unless you ask, so you must protect and honor them as they have always done for you.

Once you have mastered how to have necessary interactions with strangers, make friends and forge alliances, you will be at a point where you will start to experience for yourself what introverted balance feels like, and that means you will be ready to commit to the personal and or professional goals you've always dreamed of but never imagined you could accomplish. Goals you can easily aspire to now that your personal and professional intrapersonal support system has been securely set in place.

Personal and Professional Growth from Within

I'm a huge teacher and advocate for personal growth. Thanks to my work with my co-writer, Helen Glasgow, I've also learned to transfer the practical aspects of personal growth to the very different world of professional growth. In this book, I'm thinking out of the box once again to focus on the specific gifts as well as vulnerabilities Introverts present when faced with personal and professional growth. Can I just say, after reviewing what we've worked on so far, how much of an advantage Introverts begin with? Normally when I work with clients who are seeking personal growth coaching, the first thing we have to establish is what they are dissatisfied with and what, specifically they want to change and/or develop. Having researched and worked with introverts for this book, I have been astonished at the clarity you guys have when it comes to these two building blocks. Because your inner life and reflections are so rich and detailed, you often know exactly what's troubling you and precisely what you'd like to change or develop. Also, my training segment on the benefits of learning how to be alone and how to enjoy solitude is completely superfluous when it comes to introverts. Nope. The problems introverts are challenged with when it comes to personal and professional growth are all implementation focused.

In the past when I have taught personal and professional growth I've built the techniques around specific personality factors that determine which techniques will resonate with an individual. In this book, we can easily use the four types of introversion to find resonation. Since introverts have such a great grasp on the issues they wish to tackle, we can skip how to write inspirational and motivational statements as well as specific aspirational goals.

What I want each of you to do is to write a visionary statement, disclosing every last detail of what you are currently dissatisfied with, as well as the growth and change you wish to see. Then I want you to list every fear and roadblock you can think of that would hinder that change and growth. From there I want you to organize two prioritized lists like we did earlier in the fear section of the book, and brainstorm solutions for both the annoying, frustrating fears and the ones that hinder happiness and growth.

Now that you have a fear-free path, I want you to design your support system, including friends, allies and potential strangers you may have to interact with to meet your goals.

With this in hand we can add some additional tools:

Using Your Specific Type of Introversion to Organize Your Plan of Attack

Here's why you need to factor in your introversion type when planning how to implement your personal growth goals: say, for example you are an anxious introvert who is trying to overcome your fear of going to the gym to keep fit. How well do you think you're going to do in a cross-fit class, working out to aggressive, loud heavy metal music with buzzers going off every 90 seconds and having bulked up trainers barking orders and screaming at the people who are flagging to "hit the deck and give me 20? I'm so sorry if you are an anxious introvert and you have had to stop reading this because you are hyperventilating. What if instead, you were enrolled in a lower key program that focused on progressive yoga poses and stretches with therapeutic breathing in a darkened room with soft music or tinkling wind chimes? You get my point.

I am going to list all four introvert types once again and give advice and suggestions on how to pair them up with appropriate methods and activities you can utilize when implementing your personal and/or professional growth development.

Social Introverts: Able and at times willing to participate in social gatherings, but prefers small groups of friends and lots of solitude, people who are social introverts often display sudden energy depletion and even shut down when they have misjudged their tolerance for extroverted activity. Appropriate methods and activities for this personality factor would include journaling, scheduled action plans, activities with rules, regulations and good boundaries, structured projects with a balance of solo and small group participation, training for marathons or triathlons, competitive individual sports, furniture making, cooking and online language immersion programs.

Thinking Introvert: Characterized by a rich and imaginative inner life people who are thinking introverts are often deep in thought, tend to be unaware of what is going on around them and employ creativity in all their ventures. Appropriate methods and activities for this personality factor would include any activity that has an element of exploration, individual creativity or discovery to it, such as hiking and foraging in nature, long distance running or swimming, solving problems in a volunteer capacity, or working with at-risk children on art projects, alternative therapies, spirituality, art and music therapy or storytelling.

Anxious Introvert: Anxious introverts become apprehensive as a social event nears, often cancel at the last minute or become ill, suffer through the event if they do attend, and agonize after the event, worried that they did or said something inappropriate. Their ability to self-charge and their incredible attention to detail is often overwhelmed and overshadowed by their crippling anxiety. Appropriate methods and activities for the anxious introvert would include private therapy, one-on-one activities, and light therapy, massage to relieve stress, meditation, guided imagery, creative writing, painting, composing, photography, gentle yoga, positive thinking, Ted Talks, healing touch and Reiki.

Restrained Introvert: Characterized by a slower reaction time and the tendency to pause before they speak, restrained introverts are often unique individuals, who are quite comfortable in their skin, but would sometimes like to be better understood, accepted for they are and feel safe enough to be vulnerable. Appropriate methods and activities for restrained introvert would include wilderness retreats, ecotourism, mindfulness, research projects, myofascial release and trigger point therapy, writing, heritage crafts, historical reenactments, ancient languages, acupuncture, puzzle solving, cupping, gourmet cooking and volunteer work for social justice.

Conflict Resolution

One of the most powerful weapons an introvert can utilize when implementing personal or professional growth goals is conflict resolution. Other people and the energy they impart, can impact an introvert very powerfully, especially if the energy is chaotic or negative. The ability to understand how to diffuse this energy caused by situational, relational or transitional disruptions is what conflict resolution is in a nutshell. Situational disruptions are caused by one major, or a series of, event(s) that creates an environmental disturbance and effects anyone within that environment. War or a hurricane are extreme examples of situational disturbances. Relational disruptions are caused by a conflict between 2 or more people and can have a trickle-down effect on people related to the original group, even to the point of carrying down through generations. An acrimonious divorce or taking care of an addicted sibling are examples of relational disruptions. Transitional disruptions occur during periods of intense change such as adolescence or retirement.

Once you recognize that conflict is occurring and discern whether it is caused by situational, relational or transitional disruption, there are three basic steps to resolution:

RECONNECT/RESET/REPOSITION

Reconnect: When you reconnect during crisis resolution, you need to be in the moment and fully present to what is going on. This takes lots of energy, but it is necessary and doable if you are prepared.

Reset: When you reset, you resolve to look at the conflict through a new/fresh lens. Introverts ability to see The Big Picture usually have the ability to see innovative solutions to problems that can resolve conflict, if they feel supported enough to implement them. This is where personal support systems are so crucial.

Reposition: Once the change has occurred and the conflict has been faced, Introverts need to develop the resiliency and flexibility to move on into new territory. This is where the deconstruction of old fears comes in handy and allows the elegant and sophisticated problem-solving ability of introverts to be recognized and utilized.

For more information about this conflict resolution process, please see **The Emotional Intelligence Spectrum**.

Soft Skills

I know I've already mentioned this several times, but I can't stress enough how important it is for introverts to be cutting edge technology experts in the current work environment, especially if you'd rather have a screen to buffer face-to-face interactions. Introverts with professional growth goals that include promotion and leadership also need to take courses that teach them management and delegation skills. Learning these skills will also benefit you as an introvert with personal growth goals. Company sponsored training is a priceless bonus. The following list includes basic soft skills but is by no means exhaustive. Check in with your HR Department, in-house newsletters and training memos to stay in the know about the soft skills your workplace desires.

You might want to start with these:

Finance for the Non-Financial Manager

The Art of Delegation

Basic and Advanced Management

Advanced Excel

Team Management

Marketing Basics

Negotiation Skills

How to Protect Yourself from Manipulation

Advanced PowerPoint Presentations

Write Your Individual Growth Plan of Action

It is now time to put it all together and write a plan of action that clearly states everything you will need to do to accomplish your personal and/or professional growth goals. If you have an idea in your head, feel free to design your own Individual Growth Plan of Action. If you would like inspiration, please refer to our FREE book **The Growth Mindset** which includes an additional workbook, also at no charge, which has a complete Individual Growth Plan of Action that you can fill in.

By Joshua Moore

The Power of Introverted Leadership

I've left the subject of introverted leadership until the end of this book because to me, it feels like the culmination of all the work that has gone before it; the ultimate end-goal, if you will, of enlightened introversion.

I've known several introverted leaders in my career. One or two of them were excellent bosses, recognizing the power they had within them as well as remaining humble and therefore, approachable because they never forgot former "fears" that frustrated and hindered them. They were an inspirational example of introversion in balance.

Unfortunately, I've also known a couple of introverted leaders who were recognized, respected experts in their field, but who struggled when it came to managing people, and who in turn, were very difficult to work for. These were the unapproachable bosses, who intimidated their reports because no-one could get a handle on their temperament or how they would react to a disturbance. When their energy became depleted, which it continually did because they were fearful and stressed, employees thought they were displeased or critical of the work being done and when they shut down, which happened all too often, employees felt cut-off and dismissed, which as an indirect result of their short-circuited boss's energy blackout, they effectively were. I honestly never figured out who to feel worse for; the introverted boss or the traumatized employees... Obviously, the first example of introverted bosses were enlightened, balanced empowered introverts, while the second group...not so much. The question you may be asking, however, is WHY would an introvert, regardless of type want to take on a leadership position in the first place?

- Introverts, despite their difficulties in navigating social gatherings and extroverted energy, are born leaders because they don't depend on the energy of others to replenish their own stores.

- Introverts have the ability to see The Big Picture. In other words, they see through a director's lens.

- Introverts, once they clear up social energy fears and implementation issues, are detail-oriented visionaries.

- Introverts are elegant problem solvers

- Introverts have the innate ability for deep reflection, which allows them to see strengths and weaknesses and make the appropriate shifts in attitude to allow for improvement and growth.

- Introverts who have designed support systems for themselves are fine with being "lonely" at the top, a common complaint of extroverted leaders.

Still, for a group of people known for their

hatred of being in the spotlight...Even that is a potential plus for introverts who decide to take a leadership role. They aren't in it for the spotlight. They are motivated by their expertise in the field, their visionary approach and their desire to excel by creativity.

In an extroverted society, where the majority is clamoring to be heard, the introvert is always listening and processing. Who would you rather have led you? Someone whose biggest concern is getting attention, or someone whose biggest concern is that they've understood every detail of the situation?

There are books and articles out there that advise introverts seeking leadership roles to assimilate and take on the ways of the extrovert in order to succeed. This, in my opinion, is bad advice on several levels. First of all, one of the desirable qualities of a successful leader is to stand out from the crowd. Why then, would it be a good idea, for an introvert to try to be like everyone else? My co-author Helen is adamant that "different is good" and that in order to be picked out of the crowd for advancement and leadership responsibilities you need to focus on your professional "superpowers" rather than try to change or eliminate your weaknesses.

While it's a waste of time to try and change a weakness in order to be a better-become roadblocks to your success. Besides the universal social energy depletion issue that all introverts have to contend with in one way or another, each type of introvert has specific vulnerabilities that must be maintained in order to be a strong leader.

Professional Vulnerabilities of the Social Introvert

- Social introverts appear more "normal" than other types of introverts, so when they display the effects of social energy depletion or complete energy shut- down, their behavior can be misconstrued as dismissive, mercurial or moody. Consistent self-care, scheduled alone time and responsive and understanding support staff are necessary to mitigate those times when the social introvert leader has run out of gas.

- Because social introverts are more aware and sensitive to their energy issues, they may try to mask their deficiency by focusing on the needs of other, "squeakier" extroverts and losing their energy balance as a result. The social introvert must always remember that good leadership comes from within, and must never take a backseat to outside distractions.

- Social introverts are less tolerated than their more "obvious" introverted brethren, and because of this, when they are transparent about their social energy issues, the response can include ridicule and disbelief because they "present" as extroverts most of the time. Social introverts must rise above this reaction while making sure their needs are still met. This balance can be tricky, but as long as the social introvert is aware of and protects him/herself from the disbelievers through the self-protection techniques discussed earlier in this book, balance can be maintained.

Professional Vulnerabilities of the Thinking Introvert

- Thinking introverts get "lost in the clouds" when they are deep in inner thought – the very inner thought that produces the creative, innovative ideas that make them great leaders. The thinking introvert must ensure that s/he has a fool-proof support system in place to buffer outside influences during these crucial internal processing periods so that the thinking introvert doesn't get distracted from the important work at hand by mundane outside influences.

- Thinking introverts need to lead with their ideas and innovations, not their managerial skills. Good leadership depends on highlighting the leader's gifts, not their vulnerabilities. They are tomorrow's visionary leaders and will become inefficient and emotionally exhausted if their focus is shifted to people skills.

- It is important that thinking introverts not only practice self-protection but also utilize empathetic support systems that will also protect them from aggressive competitors with an agenda.

Professional Vulnerabilities of the Anxious Introvert

- Anxious introverts who seek leadership roles must find methods to alleviate the anxiety that overwhelms them in situations where they must interact socially, or they will be eaten alive by the judgments, real and conceived of their reports, co-workers, and superiors. As mentioned several times in this book, there are endless methods and techniques to reign in this anxiety without losing the ability to be detail-oriented and have your finger on the pulse of the industry.

- Anxious introverts must seek leadership opportunities that allow them the flexibility to work alone or with trusted allies a majority of the time. They must also learn the art of delegation so that the trusted allies can oversee and communicate the anxious-introvert's ideas and innovations.

- Anxious Introverts must protect themselves from the real and imaginary threat of being shaken off the career ladder by keeping communication open through trusted allies, rather than retreating into a corner and beating themselves up.

Professional Vulnerabilities of the Restrained Introvert

- The restrained introvert needs to be open to the potential of leadership roles that occur as a direct result of his/her passions and expertise. Because the restrained introvert is so authentic in his or her particular introversion, trying to fit in in any manner will be an epic mistake.
- Restrained introverts need to be aware that their reaction time and reticence to open up may make employees feel dismissed and distrusted. A trusted extrovert ally can help this issue in many ways, communicating for the restrained introvert, especially at the beginning stages of a project when everyone is getting to know one another.
- Restrained Introverts need to find their leadership niche, commit to it and develop

a reputation as the expert in their fields. Switching careers and jumping from job to job will emotionally exhaust the restrained introvert and rob him/her of his power and balance.

Now that the professional vulnerabilities of introversion have been identified and resolutions have been advised, we can focus on the fun part of this section. Here are some of the fields and areas where introverts can search for and excel in leadership roles:

- Publishing – Management; supervisor of copy editors and writers; production manager; promotional supervisor; head of graphic artists; senior copywriter or editor; IT specialist;
- Animal Service – Veterinarian; trainer; pet psychologist; owner of kennel or grooming facility; run shelter; management team of national or international domestic and wildlife charities; breeder;
- Online Entrepreneur – Website designer; social media specialist, blogger, run online company or service; online "soft" skills trainer, video game artist;
- Healing Arts – Run wellness center; Reiki master; acupuncturist; alternative therapy trainer; intuitive healer; coordinate seminars and festivals;

- Home Improvement – Establish niche clientele, i.e., small coordinate jobs for the elderly or disabled; interior design; styling for real-estate sales; cleaning services
- Social Justice – Coordinate events; online support, media sources; promotions;
- Adventure Companies – White water rafting, tubing, glamping, mountain biking; mountain climbing; helo-skiing; ecotourism and volunteer/vacations; scuba diving;
- Food Services – Bakery; gourmet foodie shop; caterer; food trucks; food fair coordinator; organic specialist; nutritionist; organic farming; run farmer's market; private chef;
- Physical Fitness and Rehab – Manage physical therapy site; cardio rehab; personal trainer; athletic coach and/or trainer, sports therapy; water therapy;
- Mental Health Field – psychiatrist; psychologist; researcher; drug developer.

Careers Geared Toward Specific Introvert Types:

Social Introvert: Engineering; Database Administrator; Private Investigation; Interpreter or Translator; Commercial Diving Company;

Thinking Introvert: Fashion Designer; Animation; Video Game Designer; Screenwriter; Disney Imagineer; Reality Television show concept writer and producer;

Anxious Introvert: Commercial Pilot; Medical Technologist; Run Recording Studio; Statistician, Lighting Designer; Stage and Movie Set Designer;

Restrained Introvert: Physicist; Geoscientist; Biochemist; Anthropologist; Marriage or Family Therapist; Addiction Counselor.

As a final note to this segment, if you need one more bit of inspiration to take on a leadership role, remember this: If you are the leader, you have more control over your career. Introverts need to know they are in control and what is expected of them. If you work for someone and have to answer to a "higher power", you lose at least some ability to control how your day goes. At the whim of another person, you can be directed to change course at the drop of a hat, switch gears and without warning, enter a room full of people that you have to interact with, with no clue of when you can take a break or escape for a mental recharge! I'm not saying that as a leader, all your introversion issues will magically disappear, but whatever happens, you will be able to have much more input and decision-making abilities when you are in the driver's seat.

To my way of thinking, if you've taken the trouble and effort to read this book and embark on the path of enlightened introversion, you might as well continue your journey toward empowered leadership.

The Positive Outcomes of Enlightened, Empowered Introversion

When I began this book, my primary intention was to invite people who either knew or had a feeling they might be an introvert, to explore, always with a positive focus, what that state of being actually meant. I was purposeful in my mission to go beyond the extrovert-centric stereotypes and socially negative connotations of the word "introverted", and once I'd dispelled these inhibiting myths, it was my goal to celebrate all types of introversion, including their strengths and vulnerabilities.

I wanted to eliminate the words "shy" and "afraid" from any description of introversion by deconstructing the meaning of these words and what they really signified. It was also my fervent wish to give concrete solutions to problems arising from these words, i.e. I wanted to teach introverts how to be enlightened enough to explain that being quiet is not always being shy, and empowered enough to face their "fears" and resolve them.

I like the line of this book. I feel like it has followed a logical, yet flowing path from recognition and identification to specific characteristics of the four types of introversion. From there we've tackled resolving fears, self-protection in the workplace and the home, and how to deal with strangers, make friends and forge alliances. We've progressed to finding the balance between the quiet solitude introverts crave and the social interaction they want and need so that we could look ahead at the potential for personal and professional growth, armed with a better understanding of conflict, disruptions, and resolutions. Finally, we've reached what I believe is the logical conclusion of empowered leadership for the enlightened introvert, with its accompanying vulnerabilities, benefits, and ultimate freedom.

Here are a few of the positive outcomes I believe can be achieved through enlightened, empowered introversion:

- The ability to view being introverted as a special gift, rather than a disability.
- The ability to be authentic to one's introversion without shutting the door on the rest of the world.
- The ability to resolve long-present fears and to differentiate between fears that are annoying or frustrating, and fears that hinder happiness and growth.
- The ability to interact with strangers, on an as needed basis allowing the potential to exist that these strangers may become friends or allies.
- The ability to make true, loyal friends and have meaningful relationships.
- The ability to forge personal and professional alliances, including other

introverts as well as sympathetic extroverts, who can then be implemented as the foundation of a well-designed and customized support plan.

- The ability to enjoy social gatherings on an introverts terms, without offending others.
- The ability to succeed in the workplace, without pretending to be an extrovert.
- The ability to plan and execute personal and professional growth development through the specific lens of introversion.
- The ability to attain leadership positions in an enlightened, empowered fashion, and to thrive in those positions, gaining career satisfaction and the respect and esteem of employees, colleagues, and superiors.

I hope you have enjoyed this book and found it practical and useful as well. I encourage you to read my other book **I Am An Empath**, which explores the gifts and vulnerabilities of people who are highly in tune, empathetic, to the wants and needs of others. If you are looking for more information about Emotional Intelligence, I urge you to read the book I co-authored with Helen Glasgow, **The Emotional Intelligence Spectrum**. Finally, please download a free copy of our latest book, **The Growth Mindset**, and its accompanying workbook, Growth Games, for a thorough exploration and practical implementation of personal and professional growth development.

FREE DOWNLOAD

INSIGHTFUL GROWTH STRATEGIES FOR YOUR PERSONAL AND PROFESSIONAL SUCCESS!

amazonkindle   nook   kobo   iBooks

Windows   android   BlackBerry

Sign up here to get a free copy of The Growth Mindset book and more:
www.frenchnumber.net/growth

You may also like...
EMOTIONAL INTELLIGENCE SPECTRUM
EXPLORE YOUR EMOTIONS AND IMPROVE YOUR
INTRAPERSONAL INTELLIGENCE
BY JOSHUA MOORE AND HELEN GLASGOW

Emotional Intelligence Spectrum is the one book you need to buy if you've been curious about Emotional Intelligence, how it affects you personally, how to interpret EI in others and how to utilize Emotional Quotient in every aspect of your life.

Once you understand how EQ works, by taking a simple test, which is included in this guide, you will learn to harness the power of Emotional Intelligence and use it to further your career as you learn how to connect with people better.

You may also like...
I AM AN EMPATH
ENERGY HEALING GUIDE FOR EMPATHIC AND
HIGHLY SENSITIVE PEOPLE
BY JOSHUA MOORE

Am an Empath is an empathy guide on managing emotional anxiety, coping with being over emotional and using intuition to benefit from this sensitivity in your everyday life – the problems highly sensitive people normally face.

Through recongnizing how to control emotions you have the potential to make the most of being in tune with your emotions and understanding the feelings of people around you.
Begin your journey to a fulfilling life of awareness and support today!

By Joshua Moore

You may also like...
MAKE ROOM FOR MINIMALISM
A PRACTICAL GUIDE TO SIMPLE AND
SUSTAINABLE LIVING
BY JOSHUA MOORE

Make Room for Minimalism is a clear cut yet powerful, step-by-step introduction to minimalism, a sustainable lifestyle that will enable you to finally clear away all the physical, mental and spiritual clutter that fills many of our current stress filled lives. Minimalism will help you redefine what is truly meaningful in your life.

Eager to experience the world of minimalism? Add a single copy of **Make Room for Minimalism** to your library now, and start counting the books you will no longer need!

By Joshua Moore

FN№

Presented by French Number Publishing
French Number Publishing is an independent
publishing house headquartered in Paris, France
with offices in North America, Europe, and Asia.
FN№ is committed to connect the most promising
writers to readers from all around the world.
Together we aim to explore the most challenging
issues on a large variety of topics that are of
interest to the modern society.

FN№